TABLE OF CONTENTS

Write Service and Write Your Own Paycheck

Make Up To $100,000 a Year

With No Degree!

Jeff Cowan

Write Service and Write Your Own Paycheck!

Make Up To $100,000 a Year With No Degree!

Jeff Cowan

ISBN: 978-1-54391-825-0

Copyright © 2017 by Wm. Jeff Cowan

Jeff Cowan's PRO TALK, Inc.Rancho Santa Margarita, CA

www.thejeffcowan.com

Ordering Information:

For details, contact the publisher at the address above.

Printed in the United States of America

First Edition

PREFACE

As you advance through this manual, it is my hope, as the author, to provide you with all the tools necessary to make you the absolute best you can be. The opportunity you have by working in the automotive service industry and its many talented people is one that has the potential to deliver a life, and lifestyle that can firmly place you in the top fifteen percent of income earners in North America. To make that happen you have already taken the most important step in this journey. The step of investing in yourself and your career. I will make every effort to see to it that you are successful at the highest levels in every aspect of any role you pursue with whatever company you work with. However, your ultimate success will rely heavily on your ability, willingness, and internal desire to succeed.

If you chose to succeed, it will be as easy as mastering the tools and techniques that are going to be delivered to you throughout this guide. I have made it my mission to make these tools and techniques as easy and simple to follow as possible. I can guarantee that I have gone to great lengths to make sure that everything in this manual, including techniques, methods, and processes, have been used with maximum success when applied as designed. Thousands of professionals in your field have used these same methods over many years and have found them to deliver on every point and they will for you too. Let's get started.

WRITE SERVICE AND WRITE YOUR OWN PAYCHECK!!!

Check these facts out; The *average* service advisor working in the United States today will generate enough income that will put them in the top 15% of income earners. At this rate, the *average* service advisor will have enough income to invest in a home that is about 2,300 square feet, sitting on 1.3 acres of land. The *average* service advisor will own a vehicle in the $40,000 range. If they are married and their spouse works outside the home, an additional 1,000 square feet can be added to the house they will own and another vehicle of equal or greater value. The *average* service advisor will enjoy a two-weeks paid vacation and a benefit package that rivals some of the biggest corporations in the United States. All of this, if they are *average*. Fifty percent of these advisors make well above that, earning and enjoying an even more spectacular lifestyle. Many making $100,000 and above. ***It is also important to note that most are not college graduates and most knew nothing about cars and trucks prior to starting in this field.*** They have lifestyles and incomes that the *average* college grad and American citizen can only dream about. Furthermore, the career of being a service advisor is not defined by age, race, gender or any other demographic. I have seen people fresh out of high school and some who did not even finish high school be highly successful. I have seen many in their twilight years be wildly successful. As far as gender, it's an ongoing argument in the industry as to who is the best, male or female? I have seen both experience the same levels of success. Race? Makes no difference. The only thing will make a difference is ones' inner desire to be the best they can be and have what is available to any and all takers; a career that delivers security, enjoyment, pride and an outstanding lifestyle for both self and family.

You are smart for investing in this manual and course. By doing so, you are really investing in yourself and your future. There are several characteristics employers look for in when looking for new employees; do they show initiative? Are they proactive? Do they believe in themselves? By you investing in this course you have answered those questions and several others with a big resounding YES! What this course is going to show you is how to do a job and start a career that will deliver unlimited satisfaction and the potential to have an income that will place you firmly in the top 15% of income earners in the United States and, if you choose, even higher than that.

This guide will teach you not only how to be a service advisor, but how to become the most wanted and sought-after service advisor anywhere. On any given day in the United States alone, there are over 120,000 places a person can take their vehicles for service and repair. In addition, there are a few thousand more places that exclusively handle business fleet vehicles, heavy equipment vehicles and recreational vehicles. There are also a couple thousand places that service only motorcycles. All of these places hire and employ service writers or service advisors (same thing). For every one of these places, they have an average of three service advisors. What are service advisors? Service advisors are the highly paid employees that greet a customer at a service center that has a vehicle that needs service or maintenance, finds out exactly what they need, writes it up, gets the vehicle in the shop for the customer so that a technician/mechanic can diagnose the concerns of the customer and then contact the customer and *sell* them on the solution that will make their vehicle and keep their vehicle running great.

There is just one major problem. On any given day in the United States alone, over 30,000 of these service writer seats are empty. Empty because the employers can't find people willing to do the job. Even more interesting, half of the service writers doing the job would be replaced if employers could find not only people who wished to do the job, but could do it well. In short, there is a lot of opportunity in this high paying and rewarding field.

So, if it is such a great career and pays so well, why is it so hard to fill these positions? First, most people do not know to look in this field for this great opportunity and second, it's the automotive business. The automotive business has a bad reputation, undeserved, but a bad reputation none the less for years. Let me address that. While it is true that there are those in this business that do unethical things, it has been my experience that the percentage of those who do these things is not any higher or lower than any other industry. Second, the bad reputation stems from a business that up until about fifty years ago was highly unorganized and not very regulated. But over the past fifty years, it has become significantly more organized and is now so heavily regulated, that ripping someone off or doing anything unethical is nearly impossible. Couple that with the fact that everything is now driven by a very watchful internet where delivering unethical service will be posted and will put you out of business in a heartbeat. Todays automotive business is as clean and ethical as nearly every other big business out there. It may have taken 125 years to get this point, but the industry is now safe and clean and a great place to have a career. As a matter of fact, I believe that over the next decade, the automotive industry will be one of the most sought-after places to have a career in north America if not around the world. In many ways, it already is. Besides, what do you think really matters anyway, saying you work in an industry that has an outstanding level of public acceptance but pays nothing or that you work in a business that is ethical, is respectable and does pay many six figures a year? I don't know about you, but I will take the high pay, take a great vacation with my family to some beautiful tropical island while I pay someone to watch my house and pets while the others sit in their living rooms watching the travel channel and seeing others living the dream. Couch or beach? Renter or homeowner? Economy car or luxury car? Worry or security? Mounting debt or a savings account? No contest. I will take the later in every one of those questions.

So, what do the people who are in this career and highly successful at it do that makes them so successful? They follow a very easy process, a process I will show you. *They are specialist at handling customers the correct way.* (Side Note: The number one skill shop owners look for in service advisors is people skills. The number one thing most service advisors don't have are people skills. That is why it is so easy to be great in this field. Master the techniques I show you and you will succeed in a big way.) They invested in themselves and in their selling careers, and they believed in and are now realizing the true American dream. For many, this will be their life-long and very rewarding career. Others will work even harder, sharpening their skills even more, developing new skills, and move up the ladder to even greater heights.

Whether you choose to remain as an advisor or aspire to management and beyond within the automotive industry, you have already taken the most important step by entering into what is a reputable, highly rewarding, and fulfilling career as a service advisor and sales professional. You are on the road to earning and enjoying what others will only fantasize about. You will soon be living the American dream! Furthermore, with what I teach you here, you can apply it outside the automotive industry and have equal or greater success in most industries as my processes and techniques are applicable to most every business that exist.

Hold on! Are you ready for this? Here comes the icing on the cake! If you follow my process you will be successful. If follow my process and become successful like most do who follow it, you will never be unemployed in the United States again unless you chose to be. I will show you not only how to do the job, but what metrics employers are looking for and how to exceed their every expectation. Most who use my process find themselves in the top seven percent of this field. When you do that, you will be able to go into most any town, any time, walk into just about any service center and be hired on the spot. Shoot, if you can just get yourself in the top fifty percent of the field, you are likely to be hired on the spot.

As you move forward, I don't want you to just read this manual, I want you to consume it and absorb it until you and my process become one. Take notes, reread sections, role-play, memorize and study hard. I will load your mind and your lips with all the things you need to do to get started and enjoy this outstanding opportunity. And by the way, if you like what you read and want to take another step, sign up for my online courses. If you take those courses and pass the online test, I will certify you, place your name on our national certified advisor list. I will then be directing service centers from all across the nation to visit so that they can find you and see how prepared you are to be employed by them. Either way, whether just read the book or go online, either method will set you further down the road that you just turned on, the road to a highly gratifying, highly rewarding career that will enable you to have the lifestyle you want and so desire. You are on the highway to becoming a world class service writer and a world class sales professional.

Sincerely,

Jeff Cowan

GETTING THE CUSTOMER INTO YOUR STORE

Getting the customer into the store starts from your first point of contact. Although that first point will usually happen over the phone, it can literally take place anywhere. It is important that you learn from the beginning how to sound like a professional, no matter where you are or who you are speaking with. One of the ways a customer can quickly detect your level of professionalism is by the words you chose. What follows are two lists of words:

Words to banish

Replacement words

The Professionals Vocabulary

WORDS TO BANISH	REPLACEMENT
R.O.	**Form**
Contract	**Agreement**
	Paperwork
Price	**Investment**
	Participation
	Agreement
	Fee
Deal	**Opportunity**
Complaint	**Area of concern**
Problem	**Challenge**
Sign	**Approve**
	Authorize
	Endorse
	OK
	Get your autograph
Appointment	**Check-in time**
	Reservation
Pitch	**Present**
	Demonstrate
Buy	**Own**
Sell	**Help them get**
Mechanic	**Expertly-trained technician**
Service Advisor	**Expertly-trained service advisor**
Parts	**Name-brand parts and products**

Replace **R.O.** (Service Advisor slang for repair order/work order) or **contract** with the words **form, agreement,** or **paperwork**. Why? Because people do not know what the term **R.O.** means and if they do not understand what you are talking about, they will not buy. **Contract** is bad because most people have been told by their parents that **contracts** are to be avoided and approached with caution. The replacement words are easy to understand and have no negative connotations.

*"Follow me over here, and we will get the **paperwork** completed."*

Replace the word **price** with **investment, participation, agreement** or **fee**. Price reminds people that they are spending money. The replacement words make it sound like it is just the next step in the process.

*"Your total **investment** would only be $899."*

Replace the word **deal** with **opportunity**. Deal suggests that there may be room for negotiation. There is an "up" and a "down" side to a **deal**. **Opportunity** implies that this is truly something that is one of a kind and unique. There is only an "upside" to an **opportunity**.

*"I have a great **opportunity** for you today. Invest in _____ and get _____."*

Replace the word **complaint** with the phrase **"area of concern."**

*"The **area of concern** that needs to be focused on is____."*

Replace the word **problem** with the word **challenge**. A **problem** is difficult. A **challenge** is situation that can be overcome with the right combination of events.

*"The **challenge** you are going to have is_____."*

Replace the word **sign** with the words **approve, authorize, endorse, OK,** or the phrase "**get your autograph**." The big problem with the word **sign** is that from the time you're a little tike, your parents told you to never **sign** anything without questioning or reading the fine print first. In short, it slows down the process with questions the customer does not need answered in order to move forward. It wastes time. By using one of the other words, you will rarely provoke any negativity and the customer will simply **authorize** the document.

Replace the words **appointment** and **reservation** with the term **check-in time**. The words **appointment** and **reservation** have come to mean NOW. Since a customer's vehicle rarely enters your shop at the exact time of their **reservation** or **appointment**, the customer becomes defensive when they must wait. **Check-in time** suggests a range. There is a general understanding that there will be a wait. You may have a **reservation** to fly at 7:00, but the airline request you arrive two hours early to **check-in**.

Word track for establishing the check-in time

"Mr./Ms. Customer, now that we have established your check-in time for 9:00 am tomorrow, allow me to take a moment to explain to you what that means and what will happen once you arrive. First, you will want to be here as close to your check-in time as possible. Getting here early means you will need to wait and getting here late could result in you losing your place in line. Once you arrive, your expertly-trained service advisor will be ready for you with all the information you just gave me. During the first part of the check-in process they will go over all this information to ensure that I wrote everything down correctly, to make sure they understand what your concerns are, and to see if anything needs to be added to your list. The second step in the check-in process is when you and your expertly-trained service advisor walk around your vehicle to collect numbers off your vehicle and do a quick visual inspection. The third part of the check-in process will determine which department and which expertly-trained technician will be the one best suited to diagnose and repair your vehicle. That decision will be based on what you and your expertly-trained service advisor discussed and saw during the earlier part of the check-in process. Once that is determined, we will look at the schedule for that department and the expertly-trained technician and that will determine approximately when your vehicle will enter our state-of-the-art shop."

With this word track you prepare the customer for what is going to happen when they arrive at the shop as well as how it is going to happen. You are setting the expectations which will guarantee that you will meet and exceed those expectations. It will eliminate the arguments that ensue when you allow the customer to assume what is going to happen. It is your job to define the expectations of the customer.

As an advisor, once your customer has arrived and after you have greeted them, you need say the following:

"Mr./Ms. Customer, thank you for arriving on time to get your vehicle checked-in. Now that you are here, let me explain to you what we will be doing to get your vehicle fully checked-in. First, I will be reviewing with you all the information you gave us on the telephone to ensure that it was written down correctly and that I understand your concerns. We can add anything that needs to be added. Once that is done, we will both walk around your vehicle to collect some numbers from it and to do a quick visual inspection. Then, based on what we discuss and what we see during the visual inspection, we will select the department and we will determine which expertly-trained technician will be the best to address your concerns today. Once that has been decided, we will review their schedule. This will dictate approximately when your vehicle will enter our state-of-the-art service department."

With this word track, you explain what is going to happen, when it is going to happen, how it is going to happen, and who is going to be involved. This is how you assure that everyone is on the same page. It shows the customer that you know what you are doing, that you are a professional, and that you can, and will, deliver each time they do business with you.

After you complete the first two steps that you described in the previous two word tracks, you will follow with the word track provided below:

"Mr./Ms. Customer, now that we have reviewed your original concerns and have conducted our visual inspection, I believe the department/expertly-trained technician that would be best to diagnose and repair your vehicle will be _____. Currently, they are working on another customer's vehicle. It is likely that your vehicle will be entering our state-of-the-art facility at approximately _____. Let's give them about one hour to an hour and a half to complete your diagnosis. You can expect a telephone call from me between _____ and _____ with an update on the status and findings regarding your vehicle. Fair enough?"

Finally, with this word track, you further prove that if you say it is going to happen, it will happen, exactly as you describe, every time. You are building trust. This trust will make the customer comfortable investing in more products and additional services from you. Most importantly, you continue to control the customer's expectations.

More words to replace

Replace the word **pitch** with the words **present** or **demonstrate**. Few words will make you look more like a shyster then the word **pitch**. Politicians and con artists **pitch** their products. Professional salespeople **present** or **demonstrate** them.

Replace the word **buy** with **own**. People do not like to **buy** things, but they love to own them.

"Allow me to show you how you can own these new tires."

Replace the word **sell** with the phrase "**help them get.**" People do not like to feel that they are being sold a product, but they love when a professional "helps them get it." It makes them feel more in control.

"Mr. Customer, let me 'help you get' these new tires."

Replace the word, **mechanic** with **expertly-trained technician**. Replace **service advisor** with the term **expertly-trained service advisor**. Replace the word **parts** with the term **name-brand parts/products**. Independent and second rate shops have advisors, technicians, and off-brand parts. But you work for a professional company as an expertly-trained service advisor that has **name-brand products** that are explained, installed, and repaired by **expertly-trained technicians**.

Use these three word tracks to boost your professionalism and enhance the customer's perception:

"I am an expertly-trained service advisor. I have been trained by our name-brand suppliers to work specifically with vehicles just like yours. I will work with more vehicles, just like yours, today than our competition will in the next 30 days. I have been trained to know what to look for, what to look at, and what questions to ask. This allows me to make sure that when your vehicle enters our state-of- the-art shop, it will get to the right expertly-trained technician, which will ensure that your vehicle will be worked on in the most efficient and economical way possible. This will save you both time and money. When we deliver your vehicle back to you, you can rest assured that it will be safe, reliable, and economically sound."

"Mr./Ms. Customer, all of our technicians are expertly-trained. What this means is that they have been trained and continue to be trained by the manufacturer that originally built the products we will be installing today (only say if you are working at a automotive dealership). They are constantly updated and trained on what to look at, what to look for, and how to execute a repair in the quickest, most economical way possible, saving you both time and money. They will work on more vehicles like yours today, vehicles that drive on the same roads and under the same conditions, than our competition will in the next 30 days. They are literally experts and the best at what they do."

Every part that we use is brand-name designed and engineered. Our parts are built by the same people who completely understand your vehicle which ensures that every part is a perfect fit.

We use only brand-name designed and engineered parts because we know how they will perform and because they come with a full warranty from the part manufacturer. In short, we only use the best because we feel both you and your vehicle deserve the best."

These very important word tracks tell the customer exactly who is working on their vehicle, how you as a service advisor and these technicians were trained, and how the parts were developed. It lets the customer know that your company is a truly professional organization that cares about its customers and the value each one receives.

THE PROFESSIONAL APPROACH AND GREETING

There is an old saying that goes, "You only get one chance to make a great first impression." Few things are truer. The following steps regarding the *professional approach and greeting* may seem obvious or basic, but these important steps are often over-looked and not practiced by the non-professional. It takes discipline to use these with every customer and a true professional possesses that discipline. Review, learn, and put into practice the following eight steps to make sure you get off on the right foot:

STEP 1

Smile – Smiling lets the customer know that you are relaxed, confident, and ready to address their concerns. Regardless of what is going on around you, before greeting any customer, make sure you have a smile on your face.

STEP 2

Be Enthusiastic – Enthusiasm is infectious. The more you are enthused with your customers the more enthused your customers will be to do business with you.

STEP 3

Be Confident – Confidence stems from being prepared. Being prepared means having full knowledge of your products. It also means having answers and solutions for all your customer's questions.

STEP 4

Be Relaxed – This takes discipline. Sometimes being a service writer comes with a lot of pressure and demands firing from multiple sources. The more prepared you are to handle those pressures, the easier it will be to relax and stay relaxed. When you feel tense, customers will sense it and become cautious.

STEP 5

Establish Eye Contact – Looking someone in the eye shows that you are honest, that you are listening, that you care, and that you are a problem solver. Just like in the movies, those who have shifty eyes are generally seen as dishonest and not to be trusted.

STEP 6

Offer Your First Name – Notice it says "first" name and not "full" name. By giving both your first and last name the customer will miss the first, trying to hear the last, and miss the last, trying to hear the first. If the customer cannot remember your name, they cannot ask for you on future visits. If you give your first name only, they will hear it, remember it, and will be far more likely to ask for you in the future.

STEP 7

Use the Military Rule – The Military Rule is where you simply address everyone one as Mr. or Ms. Avoid trying to get on a first name basis with customers. Show that you are a true professional and keep things business-like. In this type of fast paced sale, you will find it works to your advantage to stick to the basics of Mr. and Ms. These two titles are offensive to no one and seen as polite and professional by all.

STEP 8

Handshakes – This is another area where popular society disagrees. However, you must never forget that you are a professional salesperson serving the public. I have met and worked thousands of top salespeople. All the top professionals have a firm, confident handshake.

ASKING DIAGNOSTIC QUESTIONS

Asking diagnostic questions allows you to save time by helping the factory-trained technician 'zero in' on what the customer's concerns may be. It makes you look more knowledgeable and professional, while at the same time, helps you to build trust and confidence with your customers. Asking diagnostic questions helps you eliminate objections that take time, are hard to later overcome, and which in some cases, may not be overcome at all. By asking diagnostic questions, it increases overall productivity, customer satisfaction scores, and customer retention levels.

NOTE: Although there may be a simpler way to ask the following questions, they are asked the way they are presented so that we learn not only about the customer's concerns, but about the customer, as well. Also, note that you may need all of these questions with one customer, half of them with another, and all of them plus more with the next. Each situation is different and may require different questions. The following are just a sample and are presented to give you an idea of how to approach these questions:

*"Since you brought the vehicle in, I am **assuming** that you are the **primary** driver. Is that correct?"*

Assuming they are the primary driver is complimentary. Asking outright can be insulting.

*"Is the **primary** driver here?"*

Only ask this if the customer answers "no" to Question #1. Also, if the primary driver is not present, it needs to be made clear to the person dropping-off the vehicle that work cannot be started without contact from the primary driver/owner.

*"I am assuming that I will be contacting you throughout the day to give you **updates** and get **final approvals** on any needed services or repairs. Is that correct?"*

Just as with Question #1, **assuming** that you will be contacting the person you are speaking with, gives them prestige and power. Asking the question, "Who should I be contacting throughout the day with information about the vehicle?" is condescending and implies that the person you are speaking with does not have the capability to make decisions.

*"Mr./Ms. Customer, you said you were bringing your vehicle in today because you needed an oil change and **what else**?"*

Even though the customer has already indicated their primary concern, by not repeating it back to them, and instead, forcing them to repeat it, you will get the customer talking. This will provide greater detail about their main concern and possibly others they may have forgotten. If you simply repeat back the primary concern, the customer tends to just agree with no further explanation.

"Mr./Ms. Customer, **how long** *has it been since you first noticed this problem?"*

Possible responses and their meaning:

Customer: *"It just started a few minutes ago and I saw your store and thought I should get in here quick!"* This response is a strong indicator that the customer has very little knowledge about their vehicle and how it works. This would be a time to use phrases like *"As you may not know"* or *"What we have found"* or *"You are going to want us to _____"* in your presentation.

Customer: *"It actually started about a month ago. I knew it wasn't any big deal, so I just waited until I had time to stop in to get it taken care of and today is that day!"* This response most likely means that either the customer knows a lot about vehicles and how they work or that they *think* they know a lot about vehicles and how they work. Either way, this would be a time to use phrases like *"As you know"* or *"As you have seen before"* or *"I'm sure you know"* during your presentation.

NOTE: Either type of customer is likely to say "yes" today and is likely to say "yes" to everything, if you handled them according to their knowledge.

6. *"Do you notice it happening at any particular **time of day**? For instance, does it happen in the morning, on the way to work, on the way home from work, only at night, etc.?"*

*"Do you notice it being affected by **weather conditions**? When it is hot, cold, windy, rainy, dry or …?"*

*"Do you notice it happening under specific **driving condition**, such as on highways, side streets, city streets, country roads? High speeds or low speeds?"* Always ask the customers to define high or low speed since those terms are based on individual standards. *"When turning, driving straight or…? Does it happen when you are at a stop?"*

*"Mr./Ms. Customer, based on the information you have given me, it seems the vehicle is doing this when it is cold, at lower speeds, and that it has been doing this for a few weeks and seems to be only getting worse. Do you have any **thoughts**, **ideas**, or **direction** you would **point us toward**?*

NOTE: The secret to making Question #9 work is that you must "beat around the bush" and take your time asking the question. The more time you give the customer to think about what you are asking, the better and more telling the answer will be.

"Why do you think that is?"

NOTE: With Question #10, the sooner and more directly you ask the question, the better the answer will be. Question #10 is trying to uncover why the customer is thinking what he/she is thinking. What is his/her knowledge based upon?

CONVINCING YOUR CUSTOMER THAT THEY ARE IN THE RIGHT PLACE

To this point, you have **taken control of the customer** by **professionally greeting** them, clearly **defining expectations**, and **masterfully uncovering their issues and concerns.** The very next step and the only thing your customer will care about at this point is finding out whether or not you can solve their problems. Can you get the job done? Until you assure them that you can and will do the job, your customer will not listen to any other suggestions or presentations you make. If you want them to continue to listen to you and buy extra needed services, you must convince them prior to presenting any extras that their primary concern will be taken care of. The best way to do that is by stating the following immediately after completing your diagnostic questions:

The "Buy A Suit" Technique

"Mr./Ms. Customer, based on the information you have given me, I want you to rest assured that once our expertly-trained

technicians get the opportunity to inspect your vehicle, and/or hook your vehicle up to our latest computerized diagnostic equipment, they will be able to find the problem. As a matter of fact, I don't even want you to concern yourself with it any further, until I call you later today with the results."

Customers love to hear this from sales professionals simply because it eases their mind and lets them know that they are working with someone that has confidence, is in control, and gets things done.

This will only work on smaller, easier, quick jobs. When a service is going to be extensive and take longer, use the following word track:

The "Buy a Suit for the Big Job" Technique

"Mr./Ms. Customer, based on the information you have given me, I want you to rest assured that once our expertly-trained technicians get the opportunity to inspect your vehicle and/or hook it up to our latest computerized diagnostic equipment, they will be able to find the problem."

"That said, I want to point out that, although I am not an expertly-trained technician and cannot tell you what is causing your primary concern by simply walking around your vehicle, I can tell you based on my experience of helping many customers with matters like this, that what we are looking at here is not going to

be an easy or quick repair. I can all but guarantee you that what we are looking at will take at least all day to complete and could easily turn into an overnight stay for your vehicle, or longer."

"I also want you to know that you could not have taken your vehicle to a better place for this type of issue simply because no one is better at handling these types of concerns than my expertly-trained technicians. They are the best expert technicians available, anywhere. So please, do not trouble yourself with it any further, until I call you later with the results."

By using this beefed-up word track, you are still telling them that you will get it done and that you are best, but at the same time, you are telling them that just because we are the best, it does not necessarily mean it will be fast or free. Strong, easy, effective.

BUILDING RAPPORT

Many feel the true secret to being successful in selling is being a master at closing the sale. Although being a master at closing a sale is important, you will not get the opportunity to do so, if the customer does not like or trust you. **Building rapport** will help you build trust quickly and will show the customer that you are a caring human that is not merely trying to sell them a bunch of product. **In my mind, the building of rapport is the single most important step in any selling system.** If executed properly, it will deliver several things:

- It will help you gain the trust of your customers.

- It will help you understand what is truly important to your customer in terms of product benefits.

- It will allow you to build a true business relationship with your customers that will provide repeat business and high survey scores.

- It will ensure that your customers remember and recommend you.

NOTE: Building rapport requires that you have a conversation with your customer that revolves around anything *but* their vehicle.

Steps to building rapport

STEP 1

Listen- There are two types of listening:

passive listening

active listening

Passive listening is when you are talking with someone but are aware of other conversations going on around you. You are aware of people entering and exiting the immediate area. You fade in and out of the conversation. **Active listening** is when you fully concentrate, understand, respond and remember what is being said in a conversation. To practice *active listening,* you must be focused on every word your customer says, how they say it, and all their facial expressions as they are saying it. You must maintain strong eye contact and only looking away or down to make notes as they talk.

STEP 2

Read and project body language- If you are serious about the sales profession or any type of customer service profession, your ability to read and project body language will be essential to your ultimate success. The best way to learn these skills is to either register for a class that teaches this skill or read a book about the subject. The best book I have seen on this topic is titled, *The Definitive Book of Body Language: The Hidden Meaning Behind People's Gestures and Expressions* by Barbara Pease and Allan Pease. If you commit to the idea that body language is critical in understanding people and developing relationships, you will find this book invaluable.

STEP 3

Be sincere- Some feel that you can fake sincerity and I believe that is true- to a point. You might get away with it for the first few minutes with a customer, but very quickly, your customer will see through your insincerity and you will lose the sale and that customer, forever. It's actually very easy to show sincerity. If your livelihood genuinely depends on making relationships (and sales is that kind of livelihood), then you are already there. You merely need to ask questions, actively listen to the answers, maintain eye contact, and engage in effective body language. If you are to be a professional salesperson, this must become second nature to you.

STEP 4

Ask questions- Who, what, when, where, why, and how, are the words your questions should revolve around. Think interview. If you read an interview or watch one on television, the interview always revolves around these questions. Once these questions are asked the interview is generally over. When asking questions, avoid the topics of sex, religion, and politics. These three topics kill sales. No matter how much you think you and your customer are on the same wavelength, discussing these subjects will quickly reveal your differences bringing unwanted emotion into the exchange. If a customer brings up one of those three subjects, listen, make no comment, and then quickly change the subject.

STEP 5

Look for badges- Badges are things that allow people to reveal topics they are most interested in talking about as the stand in front of you. There are two types of badges:

physical badges

verbal badges

Physical badges are things that may be written on your customer's hat or shirt. They can be as simple as a unique belt buckle or an usual pair of shoes. They can also be things in the customer's vehicle. Items like baby seats (people love to talk about their babies), briefcases, sporting goods, or other personal items.

Verbal badges are when people reveal things about themselves in conversations where they have little or no bearing on what they are there to see you about. For example, a customer may say something like, "I want to make sure my tires are in good shape for the upcoming football season." Whether it is football season or not, you need good tires to live your daily life. The customer only brought up football because they are likely to be big fans and want to share that with you. Why else would he bring it up? The smart professional salesperson will immediately pursue the football conversation by asking questions about football. Who is your favorite team? Why do like them?

Are they going to have a great season? If you were the coach, what would you do differently? These types of questions get the customer to open-up and share their thoughts. The expert knows, that if you listen intently to their answers, you will not only get the customer to open-up, but you can uncover what is important to the customer which will make it easier to present your products.

There are generally two reasons your customers will display badges to you; enthusiasm or dominance. It doesn't matter why they reveal their badges, it is only important that you identify the badges and seize the opportunity.

STEP 6

Let the customer shine- The brighter you let your customer's star shine, the brighter yours will shine. What I am saying here is, you will only get the information you need by encouraging the customer to talk and tell their story. If you do all the talking, you will learn nothing. In the world of professional sales, I think you should never forget that you have two ears and one mouth. I think we were designed to listen twice as much as we talk. Talking less is the surest way to become an active listener. Reading the customer's body language, making eye contact, and gaining a full understanding of your customer's needs is the key to successful communication. Successful communication leads to closed sales. Anytime a customer asks your opinion on *their badge*, you should give a quick short answer followed by four more questions from you, to them. I call this the **4 to 1 Rule**. Talk less, listen more.

NOTE: You never want to stop in the middle of a write-up and have a conversation based on a badge the customer has displayed simply because it's not necessary and you will not have the time to have the conversation, anyway. The proper time to have these conversations is while conducting walk-around inspection of the customer vehicle or as you are generating their repair order. Think multitask.

THE FOUR POINT WALK-AROUND

The following are the reasons why advisors don't do the walk-around and why that's a bad idea:

MYTH: I don't have time.

FACT: It requires no additional time to check-in a customer using the PRO TALK process.

MYTH: My customers won't let me.

FACT: If an advisor says that, it is proof that they have never been trained to be a professional salesperson. Professionally-trained salespeople know that customers will do whatever you tell them to do, if the professional salesperson is in control of the situation.

MYTH: My customers don't have money. They are poor, financially challenged, and just plain broke. It is a bad economy.

FACT: The more financially challenged a customer is, the more likely they are to spend money on their vehicle. Without a vehicle, everything stops.

MYTH: I'm not doing it because I do not want to, and there are no repercussions.

FACT: Unless your title is manager or owner, you do not have the right to create or dictate policy. The walk-around inspection substantially increases retention, survey scores, and sales, while making your job much easier and far more profitable in the process. Why wouldn't you want to do it? If you are committed to your service center and to being a professional salesperson, you are required to be physically present for the entire workday. Why in the world wouldn't you maximize you earning potential and do everything in your power to be successful?

Reasons to love walking-around the customer's vehicle

You *get to know* the customer's vehicle - Just as the customer has a personality, so does their vehicle. If you pay attention to the vehicle, you will be able to predict future needs for the customer giving them more time to plan. The more you prepare your customer and the more you shape their expectations, the more success both you and your customer will achieve.

By dong the walk-around you will not paint vehicles that you did not damage.

You will find more work - By conducting the walk-around inspection, you will find more work. If you point out the areas of concern and professionally present them to the customer, most customers will not only agree to repair all that you find, but most will PAY YOU to get it repaired for them. That is a pretty sweet "gig" if you think about it.

You do it for the customer - Customer's not only *like* the walk-around inspection, they *love* it when you take the time to make sure that their car is safe and that all their needs are identified and addressed. They eat it up!

NOTE: The only danger in performing a walk-around inspection is that...CUSTOMERS WILL REBEL IF YOU EVER STOP DOING THE WALK-AROUND INSPECTION!!

Walk-around lead-in word track

(Said after the "Buy a Suit" Technique)

"To get your "check-in" completed, what I need to do now is to collect some numbers from your vehicle. To do that, it is going to require that I walk- around your vehicle. I would like for you to follow me as I do this so that we can do a quick visual inspection. The reason for this is, if we discover anything out of the ordinary, we can discuss it and make a decision on it now. The benefit to this is that, should we find something, and I do not think we will, I won't have to bug you throughout the day with a bunch of unnecessary phone calls, or worse, not be able to get a hold of you and have you return later this week to complete things we could have addressed now. Rest assured that once our expertly-trained

technicians get your vehicle into our state-of-the-art shop, they will do a much more detailed, free, 32-point inspection, but for right now, let's get started and collect those numbers."

NOTE: The "walk-around lead-in" word track is necessary to put the customer at ease and gain their trust. It shows you have control and that you have a process.

The Four-Point Walk-Around

How to do it

- **Get the V.I.N.**
- **Sit, Flip, Pop and Look®**
- **Walk to the back**
- **Walk to the front**

Every car, every time? Every car, every time!˙

NOTE: It is important, as you conduct the *Four-Point Walk-Around,* to point out any and every flaw, as well as, the good things you see on the vehicle. This forces the customer to acknowledge pre-existing damage, eliminating the possibility for your service center to be wrongly accused of causing it. It also allows you to make the customer aware of other needs you might identify, whether you sell the products and services or not. This will build trust between you and your customer by showing them that you have their best interests at heart.

The Six-Step Presentation

What follows is a very simple benefit based presentation formula. You will find as you progress in your professional selling career, that when presenting products, simple is best. Keep in mind that different courses sometimes have a different number of steps. Do not let that confuse you. The number of steps in a presentation is based on the product you are presenting. For service advising, "Six Steps" is the magic number.

STEP 1

Identify the need - This may sound obvious, but many times advisors get caught up in "shop talk" or "shop slang" and assume that the customer knows the industry terminology. Never assume. Clearly state the customers' needs in the most basic of terms.

STEP 2

Briefly describe the repair - Don't become too technical with a customer or make your description too lengthy. You run the risk of having the customer not understand and, as a result, you will lose their attention and the sale.

STEP 3

Give the benefits - This is the single most important step of the "Six Steps." Why? Because customers will not pay money for any of your products, but they will gladly pay you money, and lots of it, for the *benefits* your products or services provide. Never assume your customer knows the benefits of what you are showing them.

STEP 4

Communicate the fee and the duration of the repair – Let your customer know how long the service or repair will take and the fee for the repair. Remember to always pad the time estimate. If you need the extra time, you will have it. If you don't, you will look fast and efficient. When presenting the fee, exaggerate it by at least ten percent. Again, this gives you extra money should something unexpected appear. It will also allow you to come in under budget, which is always a good thing.

STEP 5

Close the sale - This is one of the most common areas of weaknesses for the average service advisor. Advisors are fearful because they lack the knowledge of exactly how to ask. Furthermore, the average service advisor knows only three closes or three ways to ask for the money. I recommend that before you ever step in front of any customer and ask them for the sale, you know at least twenty different closes or ways to ask for the money. Once you have twenty closes in your arsenal, you should learn a new one every few days until you know at least one hundred ways to ask for the sale. The more closes you know, the more effective you will be.

STEP 6

Handle the objections -The average customer is likely to say "no" to your first closing attempt. Almost as many will object two, three, or more times before saying "yes." There a host of reasons for this. It could be that they do not understand, or are not seeing the value in what you are presenting. It could be that they are simply trying to get you to drop your price and surrender your commission. Every product lends itself to objections you will hear time and time again. The more you prepare for these objections, the more successful you will be.

THE ART OF SELLING FROM A DISPLAY

When selling tires, a common mistake made is over educating the customer. While it is true that a *few* customers do care about the technicalities of the tire, most customers do not. The demonstration steps and word tracks that follow will deliver optimum sales and help you to sell more of your "Best" products.

You must know your product – Not just your product, but all the products available. You must be a product expert regarding your own products and those of your competition. By the way, being a product expert means memorizing the many features, advantages, and benefits of your product. You can't claim to be an expert and need to "Google" everything, every time. You must have the information committed to memory.

Place your body at a 45-degree angle to the product – If you know your product, you should not have to look at it while you are presenting it. You need to face your customer so that you can read their body language and facial expressions.

Place your body at a 45-degree angle to the product – Assuming this posture will allow you to be able to glance at the product, should the customer point to it while asking a question.

Always start with the "Best" and give a full presentation about it - When you start with the "Best" you are likely to sell more of it.

ONLY if the customer objects do you present a "Good" product alternative – If you present your "Best" product and ask the customer to buy it, and they say "yes", start writing – it's sold!

After presenting "Good" do not stop and move right to "Better" - If the customer objects to your "Best" product, move down to "Good" and then up to "Better," giving a presentation on both.

End your presentation by restating "Good" and moving up to "Best" – See the word track below:

Close the sale by asking the customer to decide -

See the word track below:

NOTE: You always want to help the customer get the "Best" whenever possible, but even if the customer decides on "Good" they are still buying from YOU! That is a win, win.

The word tracks for selling from a display and making the "Close"

"Mr. Customer, now that we have decided you need tires *for your vehicle, I am going to show you the 'Best" set for your vehicle.* **Point at your "Best" tire.** *We consider this our "Best" because it was the tire, or type of tire, that was specifically designed for your vehicle. Since it is just like the tire that was originally installed on your vehicle, you will like it. You already know how it feels, how it will perform, and how long it will last. It will guarantee that you maintain the ride, comfort, and handling that you experienced when you first bought the vehicle. It also comes with ___ warranty that covers ___, ___, and ___. I have these in stock, they are $299 each, and I can have them expertly mounted on your vehicle in about ___ hours. Should we go ahead and do that?"*

If the customer says "yes", walk them away from the display, return to your rapport topic, and start writing up the order. You have made a sale!

If they object by stating something like, "Why would I want to give you $299 a tire when I passed at least two other places on the way here that have tires for $99 a piece?" This will be the most common objection you receive. You should immediately respond with:

"Mr. Customer, I know which tires you are talking about, and they are "Good" tires. I know they are "Good" tires because I have some just like those right here. **Point at your "Good" tire.** "They are "Good" tires because they will last for about ___. They also come with a warranty that covers ___, ___, and ___. By* *investing in these tires, you will be giving up the ride, comfort and handling you are used to, but if your budget only allows for that level of performance, then this is a "Good" tire. We have these in stock and they are $99 each.* **Do not stop talking.** *But, if you want to get closer to the ride, comfort, and handling you are used to, then you may want to at least consider getting our "Better" tire. It is a "Better" tire because it is warranted for ___ and covers ___, ___, and ___. They are $199 each, I have them in stock and could have them expertly mounted today as well.* **Do not stop talking and continue with,** *"So now that you have seen my entire line-up of tires, which would you like for me to get expertly installed today? The "Good" tire that sacrifices the ride, comfort, and handling but keeps you within your budget at $99 each; our "Better" tire that gets you closer to the ride, comfort, and handling that you are accustomed to for $199 each; or our "Best" tire that was originally designed for your vehicle. It will maintain the performance, comfort, handling, and ride that made you invest in your vehicle in the first place, at $299 each? Mr. Customer, it is your vehicle therefore it is your decision. You just tell me which one you wish to have expertly installed on your vehicle and I will make it happen.* **Now shut-up no matter how long the silence lasts and wait for the customer to choose.**

NOTE: This word track and close are brilliant. Here is why. The sales person that tries to sell tires on technical information will always sell more "Good" and "Better" tires than they will "Best" tires. They also have more complaints from their customers because the customer many times does not understand that the cheaper tires will result in poorer performance. Advisors who present to their customers using the above word-track typically sell more "Best" tires than they do "Good" and "Better" combined. They also have virtually no complaints after the customer drives away. Why? Because they are selling the one thing the customer is most concerned about, performance. This includes ride, handling, and comfort. This word track clearly explains what the customer is getting for their money. With my method, a customer who buys a lesser tire knows they are sacrificing performance. They will be less likely to complain later because you thoroughly explained all the options and they made the decision based on facts. If they do complain, you can simply remind them that the decision to purchase the tire that they chose, was theirs. Most customers will purchase "Best" tires because it does not make sense to purchase a tire that is going to cause a vehicle to underperform. The difference between investing in "Good," "Better," or "Best" tires is usually no more than one monthly car payment. Brilliant!

HOW TO ELIMINATE 85% OF "HEAT" CASES AND BAD SURVEYS

Tell the customer what is going to happen or what might happen *before* it happens and they will be completely satisfied.

Again, you can see that what I am suggesting here is to take control and set and manage your customers' expectations. By setting expectations that you can meet or exceed, you will all but guarantee your success every time. The following *"Realistic Expectations" Close* will do this for you:

The "Realistic Expectations" Close

"Mr./Ms. Customer, let me explain the timeline for completing the repair when diagnosing a concern like the one you have just described.

About 50% of the time, we can get it diagnosed, repaired, and back to you, by the end of the day. However, once we get into a repair, we may discover that it is going to take a little longer than expected or we may discover that we don't have a needed part in stock. This would mean that you would need to leave the vehicle overnight or pick it up and bring it back tomorrow when the part arrives. In rarer instances, if a needed part is not in the area or it is on backorder, you would need to pick up the vehicle and bring it back in a few days so that we can finish the repair. Unfortunately, I won't know where we stand until our expertly-trained technician gets your vehicle into our state-of-the-art shop and gets it hooked up to our computerized diagnostic equipment and/or inspects it. Once he determines what the problem is, I'll call you and let you know where we stand. Fair enough?"

NOTE: The promise-time established is stating that the work will be done sometime between now and in the future. This is a promise-time you can meet every time.

If a customer objects to the above word track or challenges you on it in anyway, it is a sign that they are trying to bully you into putting them at the front of the line or worse, trying to get you to promise something that you can't do so that when you fail, they receive a discount. I say, no way! Instead, stay in control and use the "Three Options" *Close*:

The "Three Options" Close

"Mr./Ms. Customer, first let me apologize if you feel you have been misled. That is not the way we do business. You see, no matter where you take your vehicle, they would not be able to give you a promise-time for a concern like the one you have

*described to me here today, without first inspecting the vehicle. So again, I apologize for the misunderstanding. However, we do have **three options** and I would like to explain them to you. Our **first option** is to have you go ahead and leave your vehicle today, let our expertly-trained technicians inspect it, and/or hook it up to our state-of-the-art computerized diagnostic equipment, and see what they find. If all goes well, we will find the problem, get your approval to fix it, make the repairs, and you can pick it up at the end of the day. Remember, there is a 50% chance that this is the way it will happen.*

*Our **second option** would be at your expense. We can help you get a rental vehicle, if it looks like your vehicle won't be finished by the end of the day. As a matter of fact, if you like, we could arrange that for you, now, so you will not even have to return tonight. Our **third option** would be for you to take your vehicle with you and schedule a time to come back when you can leave it for an extended period. Which of these three options do you feel is going to work best for you today?"*

NOTE: Many advisors fear using this word track because they fear that somehow they will offend the customer or make them angry. The exact opposite is true. Instead, the customer will see you as displaying leadership, control, and confidence. You are demonstrating that you have processes in place that are tried and true. Their situation is not unique or new to you. You and your company are experienced and you are confident in the processes by which you do business.

ESTABLISHING THE PROGRESS REPORT

Tell them you will call them

Allowing the customer to call you will generate three incoming telephone calls per customer, averaging a duration of three minutes each. Let's say you help 15 customers in a day, that is a total of 45 incoming telephone calls, lasting two hours and 15 minutes! By maintaining control and instructing customers to *wait* for your call, those same 15 customers will generate 20 outgoing telephone calls at three minutes each for a total of just *one* hour per day. You just saved one hour and 15 minutes of your precious time!

Give a time-frame, not a time

By giving the customer a time-frame instead of a specific time, you are making it easier to deliver the call *on-time.*

"Mr./Ms. Customer, as you know you are always welcome to call me anytime you like throughout the day with any question or

concern you may have. However, for your convenience, I will be giving you progress reports throughout the duration of your vehicle's service so that you will always know exactly where we are. For this visit, expect two. The first, between ___and ____ (insert time) *to let you know how we are coming along and the second to let you know we have completed the work so that we can schedule your delivery time, okay?"*

"Great! Remember, there is no need for you to call me, unless your contact number changes."

NOTE: You should always add progress reports for longer or bigger jobs. It is always better to call too much, rather than too little.

Following-up throughout the day

Contact information - Get a current and up-to-date phone number where the customer can be reached. This may require that you get several numbers for different times of the day. It may require you get multiple cell phone numbers and an e-mail address.

Establish contact times - Give an approximate time that your customer can expect your contact. Contact them even if there is no new news, but contact them. Also, at the end of each contact, inform the customer when the next approximate time is that you will be contacting them. Never tell your customers to "call you later." By doing so, you surrender the control of your telephone. Instead, you al*ways* contact them.

Explain the process - After giving approximate contact times, explain to your customer that if they are not where they said they would be when you do try to contact them, and if you are unable to speak with them, any, and all work will cease until contact is made. Do not be afraid to inform the customer of this. After all, they do have some responsibility here too.

Leave a specific message -If you are forced to leave a message for your customer because they were not available, give them an approximate time to return your call. By doing this, you decrease the possibility of you not being available. You may need to give a couple of options by saying something like:

"You'll be able to easily catch me between 1:00 and 1:45 or between 2:30 and 3:30. If those times do not work for you, you are welcome to try other times but it may be a little more difficult to reach me."

Giving the customer approximate times will help you maintain control of your day.

Be upbeat -When making callbacks, be upbeat. You are delivering good news. You have solved their problem. **Avoid** saying things like:

"Are you sitting down?"

"Boy, I hate to tell you what we found".

Again, this is not bad news, it's great news! You solved their problems.

"Mr./Ms. Customer, I have great news! Your expertly-trained technician was able to find the problem and he said it was_____, and by doing_____, the benefits will be_____. We will have your vehicle done in a few hours and the fee will only be $475. If I can get your approval right now, I will let your expertly-trained technician know and he will get to work on it right away. Okay?"

Schedule time for follow-up calls - Schedule times, usually 10 or 15 minute segments, where all you do is make follow-up calls. It may seem impossible some days to stick to this, but if you at least plan it this way, you will be surprised at how easy it becomes to make it work.

Don't over-extend yourself - If you, deep down inside, know that you have made an honest attempt to make all your callbacks throughout the day, by using this system or one of your own, and you *still* cannot make it happen, then it is a clear indicator that you are writing up too many customers. If this is the case, I recommend that you cut your daily write-ups back by two or three. If that does not help, maybe cut them back another two or three, or hire an assistant

BECOMING A "MASTER CLOSER"

Characteristics of a Master Closer

A *closer* **knows no stranger**. *Closers* are willing to talk with anyone at any time about their products.

A *closer* is someone who **encourages others and loves helping others.** Closers are never threatened by new hires. Instead, they help them.

A *closer* is a **goal setter.** A *closer* without goals is like a boat without a rudder.

A *closer* is a **self-starter.** *Closers* do not wait for anything. *Closers* make things happen.

A closer has more **motivation** and **ambition** than the customer has objections. That motivation and ambition stems from the intense desire to exceed their goals.

A *closer* **thrives on the art of the deal.** *Closers* know the art of the deal is solving the customer's problems. Solve the problem and the commissions will follow.

A *closer* takes care of **future needs** and gives **great service.** Every *closer* knows the meaning of truly great service.

A *closer* is in **business for themselves.**

Closers know that no one is going to care more about their personal needs and their commitments than they do. Self-reliance is a cornerstone of a *closer's* mind-set.

A *closer* knows the good and the bad aspects of their product. *Closers* **present their product in the most positive light.** A *closer* knows no other way to do it.

A *closer* can make **every product look great,** even the dullest. Everything is exciting through the eyes of a *closer.*

A *closer* knows to **never stop learning and constantly seeks out new knowledge.** *Closers* know that the day you stop learning is the day you stop growing and the day you start going backwards.

A *closer* is a **showman.** *Closers* know that a showman is someone that thinks on their feet, is ready for any situation, and has the charisma to engage the listener, no matter where or when. They are always prepared.

Facts about Closing

The average service advisor knows **three *closes.***

As an advisor, if you do not know at least 25 *closes,* you will fail. The best advisors that I have ever met know at least 100 *closes.*

The average sale over-the-phone is made on the **fourth** attempt.

If you only know three *closes,* where does that leave you? Discounting- Discounting your sale and giving away commission.

Sixty percent of *closes* are missed because no one asked.

He who does not ask, does not get the sale or the commission.

Eighty percent of all sales people have never read a sales book.

All the people we most admire in the world never stop studying their profession. Whether they are business professionals, athletes, musicians, doctors, etc., the best of the best never stop training, learning, and perfecting their craft.

Closes that work on any service drive

The "Assumptive" Close

This is one of the most basic *closes* of all time and one of the most effective. This is where the salesperson simply assumes the customer is going to buy at the end of a presentation. After all, why wouldn't they want to buy if you have presented what they asked for or what they truly need? This *close* offers a 70% plus *closing* ratio and will likely be the *close* you use first and most often. It works in most situations, with most personalities.

After making a presentation, the *closer* states something like this:

"So Mr./Ms. Customer, now that you see how we will get this taken care of and why you need it, I will go ahead and add it to the repair order."

Start writing or typing. If they do not stop you, **they have bought**! It's that easy!

The "Are You Sure?" Close

This is most used as a second option *close*. It gets the all-important "first no" out of the way and forces the customer to rethink their decision. Effective *closing* ratio- 40% on the spot. This *close* is best used immediately after a customer gives their first objection after your first *close*. To deliver this *close*, simply look the customer in the eye and ask:

"Are You Sure?"

Asking this simple question does a few things. It makes the customer think about the **validity** of their decision. It makes them realize that **you're serious** with your suggestion and that "**no**" is not a viable option.

The" Alternative Choice" Close

Although this *close* can be used in countless situations, it is best used when presenting tires, batteries, or any other product where more than one option is available. This *close* will gain an 80% or above *closing* ratio.

The secret to making this work best for you is to always make sure that the choice you offer is between **buying and buying**, and not between buying or not buying. For example:

"So now that I have presented you with all your options Mr./Ms. Customer, which option do you feel is best for you: The platinum or gold package?"

No matter how they respond, you have just made a sale. By presenting two options, you are telling the customer that "no" is not an option and that this service or product is a must. It is not a matter of *if* they are going to buy, but rather, *what* they are going to buy. Strong!

"Let Me Show You How To Protect Your Investment" Close

The best place to use this *close* is when you are presenting preventative maintenance and other menu items. This *close* is most effective on customers who keep their vehicle in meticulous shape, always clean and in order, both inside and out. This will offer a 70%-90% *closing* ratio.

You always start this *close* out by stating:

"Mr. Customer, let me show you how to protect your investment".

It is important that you say this and reference the protection of the vehicle because it will immediately capture the attention of this type of customer.

"Mr./ Ms. Customer, let me show you how to protect your investment. The engineers that designed this vehicle, along with our expertly-trained technicians who work on vehicles like yours every day, have found that rotating your tires on a regular basis will prolong the life of your tires. It will alleviate the need to purchase new tires prematurely, saving you time and money. It will allow our expertly-trained technicians the opportunity, on a regular basis to inspect other items around the wheel, making sure you and your family are safe and secure. And again, it helps you to protect this most important investment allowing you to get more at trade-in time."

Honest, direct and effective.

The "You May Not Want To" Close

This *close* is best used when a customer is argumentative or questions your integrity. This *close* should deliver a 20% *closing* ratio. Now I know a 20% *closing* ratio doesn't sound very high, especially when I told you earlier that your *closing* ratio should be 70% or higher. However, for this situation, you'll see that 20% is actually pretty good. Let me explain. Whenever you argue with a customer, who always wins? The customer, right? That produces 0% *closing* ratio. When most people argue with another person, they state their side of the issue and then shut-up to let the other person make their case. While your adversary is stating their side of the argument, you are thinking only about your comeback. If you're *only* thinking about your comeback, what are the chances that you're listening to what the other person is saying? Zero chance. Zero percent *closing* ratio in this situation. So, all of a sudden, 20% doesn't sound that bad.

Let's say that you present a service to a customer and after doing so, they respond this way:

"You've got to be kidding me! I've driven cars for over thirty years, and I've never had anybody ask me to do something like this on any car I've ever driven. I didn't need it then and I certainly don't need it now!" This sounds pretty argumentative. And not only that, but this customer has just questioned your integrity. Instead of arguing with them, use the *"You May Not Want To" Close.*

"Mr./Ms. Customer, then you may not want to. No really. You may not want to."

Please notice that "You may not want to" is said two times, and it is imperative that you say it two times. Here is why: First, the customer's comments reveal that they are expecting an argument. By *not* doing so, and agreeing with them, I've taken away the possibility of argument and this will surprise the customer. If you watch the customer closely while you say this twice, their head will slightly jerk and their eyes will slightly pop.

"Yes, that's right, I said you may not want to."

Here's the *close:*

"Mr./ Ms. Customer, then you may not want to. Really, you may not want to. But, I think I would be doing you a big disservice if I didn't explain to you what this decision means. Frankly, I have people that come in here every day with cars just like yours that need the exact same thing I just recommended to you. They too have driven cars for many years, and no one has ever asked them to apply these services. They too believe that the services are unnecessary and they decide not to have them done. They do not have the services made to their vehicle. In failing to do so, the parts that we are trying to maintain continue to wear until they completely cease to perform, causing a major breakdown which is always accompanied by a major repair bill. On the other hand, we have customers that come in just like you, needing these types of services and they understand that as cars evolve and new technologies are introduced, the way you maintain your vehicle changes, as well. They invest in the service and don't have breakdowns or major repair bills. Mr./Ms. Customer, this is your decision, and if you feel like you do not want to do this today, I will write you up for what you came in for and provide you with a description of the additional recommended services. I will make note that you declined to have the services done. So, if you'll just initial right here stating that we talked about these services and you declined them, and then sign right here, releasing

the vehicle to us, we'll get your vehicle in the shop, get your new tires mounted, and have you out of here in _____. It's no big deal."

Hold-on! You stated previously that I need to learn how to *close* sales stronger and handle objections better, and be more persistent, yet in this *close* you are suggesting that I let the customer off-the-hook? What's up with that? Well, here's the thing. If you attempt to *close* this customer after their very clear objection, you will revert to the argument posture. As I stated earlier, an argument posture will leave you with a 0% *closing* ratio. In this case, you are rolling the dice and hoping that two out of ten of these types of customers will respond in the following way:

"Wait a minute! What's the difference between this car and the cars I've driven in the past that would make me to need this service today?"

Two out of ten will almost always change their mind.

Here's something else interesting about this particular *close*. We have discovered that for every two customers who change their minds, another three, for a total of 50% *closing* ratio, will call you after leaving your store and say something like this:

"I was doing some research on my drive home and if it's not too late, I'd like to go ahead and get the service done that we talked about today."

Not bad when you think about it. Twenty percent immediately on the drive and possibly another 30% later in the day. Both are better than 0%.

The "Based On What Our Customer's Tell Us" Close

This *close* offers a 50% *closing* ratio and is best used when you have a customer that, no matter what you say, believes that you are never right. In their eyes, if you are never right, then you must not try and explain anything to them. Instead let the customers provide the testimony. It sounds like this:

"Mr./Ms. Customer, I was excited when I heard that you were coming in today, especially given your vehicles' current mileage. Over the past several months, I have had several customers come in with vehicles just like yours at about the same mileage. They discovered that by having us perform a tire rotation on their vehicle, it prolonged the life of their tires. This means they are not having to replace them prematurely, they are ensuring that they have a better handling car, a better riding car, and a car that is safer for them and their families. On the other hand, the customers who have not opted for the tire rotation are finding that their tires are wearing-out much faster and that their vehicle's performance and safety suffer. Based on what our customers are telling us, how would you like to proceed?"

This works because it is not you trying to sell the necessary service, it is previous customers who are doing the selling. Since the customers you are referencing are not present, an argument cannot ensue. In some cases, this type of customer may respond by taking a stand and stating that they are smarter than your other customers. This is one of the few *closes* that will work with this personality and will get at least 50% to buy what you present. As far as the other 50%, I think they are largely unhappy people and nothing you do will persuade them.

The "Empathy" Close

This *close* is time-tested and has a long and proven track record. It is sometimes called ***"The 3 F's Close"*** or the ***"Feel, Felt, Found Close."*** Today it is commonly referred to as the ***"Empathy Close"***, since what you are doing is showing *empathy*. Empathy is the ability to feel what another is feeling. It is having an understanding far deeper than sympathy. For whichever title is used, this *close* is extremely versatile and can be applied in a wide variety of situations. This *close* will deliver a 70% to 80% *closing* ratio depending on how and when it is used.

In this scenario, let's assume that a very good customer of yours comes in because they have a nail in their tire and they are hoping to have it repaired. As you are getting the vehicle checked-in, you notice that the customer needs a few additionally important services. After presenting this information to the customer, they respond with the following:

"I know I need to get this additional work done, you know me, I typically do whatever the vehicle needs because I clearly

understand the importance of maintaining and repairing my car.
But what you don't know is that I am having had some financial
setbacks and I'm afraid my car is not at the top of my priority list.
The only reason I came in is because of the nail in the tire. I'm
really hoping we can save it."

You should believe them. I mean, if they have been one of your
best customers and they have purchased everything in the past,
you should believe them. I do not think that your customer is
going to start lying, just because they, suddenly don't want to
buy services and repairs anymore. I would believe them. **BUT,**
this does not mean that you should avoid making sure that
your customer understands the ramifications of not applying
the services. Here you would use the *Empathy Close*:

"Mr./ Ms. Customer, I understand how you feel, others have
felt the same way, but let me tell you what we have found. As a
matter of fact, Mr. Customer, I found myself in the same position you are in right now. I knew that my vehicle needed services, but financially, things were tight. It's a bit of a dilemma.
Do you forgo the services, hang on to your money, and hope
the car holds out? Or, do you tighten your budget even more
and do the services and repairs needed to insure the depend-
ability of your vehicle? After all, your vehicle is how you get
back and forth to work so that you can right the ship. For me,
I've always sided with maintaining the car. Of course, because I
work here, I see all too often what happens when people opt out
of the service recommendations. You know what I mean?"

Over 70% of the time this close will change the customer's mind and they will go with whatever you recommend. Sometimes, just letting the customer know you have been in their shoes is all it takes to convince them to make the repairs.

The "In The Long-Run" Close

If you have been on a service drive for more than 15 minutes, I am going to assume that you have used this *close* about 100 times. This is one of the most popular and most used *closes* by service advisors. Service advisors like it simply because it works.

With this *close,* you are making a case for the long-term benefits of applying the services you are presenting. This approach and *close* will garner a 70% plus *closing* ratio and is best used when a customer states that they want to get the service but they want to wait.

For this example, let's assume that you have suggested that the vehicle in question needs tires. The customer responds with, "I think I'll wait on that." Respond with the following word track:

"Mr./ Ms. Customer, if you wish to wait on new tires you can do that, simply because it is your vehicle and your decision. But let me point-out that based on the number of miles you typically put on your vehicle in a month, and your driving habits, waiting to replace the tires sometime in the next 90 days, will result in them being completely worn-out. When that happens, you could be

looking a flat tire. Flat tires rarely happen in your driveway. A flat tire will not only mean new tires, but possible a towing bill, lost work, and impaired safety for you and your family. **In the long-run,** *you will not only have the peace-of-mind of knowing that your tires are fine, but you will have saved over $___ on a tow bill and avoided lost work. The new tires are about $____. That alone makes it worth reconsidering, wouldn't you agree?"*

What makes this work is that you state very clearly the possible consequences of their postponement of action. From time to time I will listen to *closers* using *closes* like *In the Long-Run* and it doesn't work at all because they use wishy washy statements like, "*It could happen*" or "*This might happen*" or "*It's probable*" or "*Possibly*". The problem with these uncertain phrases is that you are suggesting that possibility of waiting exists.

"Well, if it is possible that this could break, then it is also possible that it won't, right?" What do you say to that? "

You can eliminate this response by using definitive language, such as, "*It will happen*" or "*You must*" or "*It will break and fail*". You create an urgency to get the customer to buy the services, now. This *close* works because it is based on truth. If you maintain a vehicle, it will perform and be reliable, if you don't, it won't.

The "Based On Reality, Later May Be Too Late" Close

This *close* is highly aggressive and should be used sparingly. As a matter of fact, the only time I suggest using this close is when a customer is making a decision that is clearly going to affect their long-term safety and well-being. It is aggressive because when you look at a customer and say, "Based on reality…" what you are really saying is that their logic is unsound and not based on the facts or reality. This *close* will deliver a consistent 50%-60% closing ratio. The 40-50% that decline your offer after told this information are doing so I believe because they simply and truly do not have the resources to move forward.

Before I present this *close*, let me clarify the important difference between a *scare tactic* and *truth*. A *scare tactic* is a lie that a salesperson tells a customer to get them to buy something that they do not need. The *truth* is the *truth*. At times the truth can be easy and fun to talk about, but at other times it can be difficult and uncomfortable. Truth is the truth, however, and it will always stand firmly beside you and will never waver.

Let's assume that a customer needs new tires. After inspecting the vehicle, your expertly-trained technician tells you that the tires are so bad that he will not even drive-it out of the shop. You make the customer aware of this finding. They react with a resounding firm "no." The customer returns to pick-up their vehicle and you try again. Still, the answer is, "no." You physically show them how bad the tires are and still, "No, no, no!" It is now time for the *"Based On Reality, Later May Too Late" Close*:

"Mr./Ms. Customer, at this point, it makes no difference to me or anyone else in this shop where you purchase your tires. It's not about that anymore. As a matter of fact, we want you to promise us that when you leave here in a few minutes, you are going to go to one of the shops right across the street and let them put new tires on your vehicle. If you can't do that, then at the very least, promise us that you will take your vehicle home, park it in your garage, and not let anyone drive it until you can get new tires put on. Mr./Ms. Customer, the reason I implore is because you are leaving here in a vehicle that has been deemed unsafe and when I think of you and your family riding around in this car in this condition, it makes me feel very uneasy. Based on reality, Mr./Ms. Customer, later may too late."

Expect the customer to accuse you of using *scare tactics* because almost every customer will, when you speak to them in this manner. Do not cower. Do not relent. Instead, hold firm and follow with this:

"That is right, Mr./Ms. Customer, I am trying to scare you. I am trying to scare you into seeing just how bad these tires are. They have been deemed unsafe, Mr. Customer. It is not a question of "if" they are going to fail. They are going to fail and when they do, it could cause a serious accident or you could hit something. What you hit and how hard you hit it will only be determined by how fast you are going and what's in front of you at the time. Mr./

Ms. Customer, you are putting both yourself and your family in a very dangerous position and like I said earlier, based on reality, later may be too late."

After saying this, you will know you have *closed* them when they look at you and say, "*You're serious about this aren't you?*" They've bought and you should start writing or typing and say:

"Yes, I am, Mr./Ms. Customer, and now that you understand the situation, let's get your car back into the shop and get those new tires mounted."

Motion for the porter to get the car off the drive and back into the shop. It is important to not hesitate. By handling this situation in this manner, 50% -60% of customers will not stop you. Those who do probably have money issues because the fact is that customers are not dumb and they will almost always do what is right and what protects their family.

The "You'll Be Glad You Did This" Close

There are two situations for which this *close* is perfect: One is when the customer is on the edge of deciding based on safety. The other is when the customer is considering updating or increasing the vehicle's value through accessorizing. The effective *closing* ratio with this *close* is a healthy 70%-90%.

For example, let's say that you just finished presenting a set of chrome wheels to the customer and they respond by saying, "I don't know? It's an awfully big expense." You respond by saying:

"You should not look at it as an expense at all Mr./Ms. Customer but rather as an investment. An investment in updating the appearance of the vehicle, an investment in your peace-of-mind, knowing that you have a vehicle that has a fresher appearance, and an investment in the vehicle's value. Mr./ Ms. Customer, everyone knows that a vehicle with more options, accessories, and appearance packages always makes the vehicle more desirable and therefore worth more to any potential future buyers. Take it from me, Mr./ Ms. Customer, based on what I have seen, you'll be glad you did this."

Start writing or typing. If they do not stop you then you have made a sale!

By the way, what makes this *close* work for this scenario, is that when the customer expresses uncertainty about spending the money and questions the value of the investment, they are asking you for *reassurance*. By quoting facts, you provided *reassurance* that making the investment is the right decision and you are giving the customer the go-ahead to move forward. This *close* will require that you deliver with a higher level of enthusiasm than usual.

The "My Dad Always Told Me" Close

This *close* is best used with younger customers. It requires that you refer to a higher authority figure that you believe the customer respects. This higher authority can be any number of people including a dad, mom, brother, sister, aunt, uncle, boyfriend, girlfriend etc. I personally prefer my Dad, only because my Dad did what I say is done in this *close*. The *closing* ratio you should gain from this *close* is in the 60%-70% range.

After presenting a needed service to a younger customer, they respond with something like, "I'm not sure if I should do this. I just don't know." Here is the perfect time to make the following *close*:

"Mr./ Ms. Customer, I know these decisions can be tough, especially when it is your first car, but I have to tell you that whenever I have found myself in the same position you are in right now, I always remember what my dad told me from the very first time I got my very first car. He told me that no matter what was going on in my life and no matter how tough things were, the maintenance of my vehicle should always be among my highest priorities. He said it was a high priority because a car is freedom. When it is maintained properly, it runs and when it's running, it ensures the basics in life like getting back and forth to work. This is important, he said, because if I am unable to do at least that, I would be unable to provide for myself and my family. If I was unable to do the most basic things, then I was a zero. He didn't raise a zero, he told me. He told me to make certain that the car was always maintained. You know, no matter how much I hated it when he said that, and he said it a lot, looking back over the years, I know he was right. So, let's take a great dad's advice and get this taken care for you so you too can continue to accomplish the basics in your life with one less thing to worry about. Okay?"

I've used this *close* many times and with great success and you will have that same success, if you use it.

The "Why Would You Want To Do That?" Close

This *close* is most used during tire presentations. It is used anytime a customer says something that makes absolutely no sense. This *close* is effective when, say for example, a customer declines the purchase of a set of new tires when it is clear that their tires are worn-out and unsafe. Remember, customers are trained to say "no" at *least* once and most will say "no" even if their reasoning is unsound. Effective *closing* ratio 80%-90%.

You present, they decline, you say:

"Why would you want to do that?"

And SHUT UP! The secret to making this work is that you must force the customer to justify what is obviously a *dumb* decision. What is great here, and why this works, is that a *dumb* decision is indefensible. The customer won't even try to defend it. Instead they are likely to just say something along the lines of, "Ya, I guess that would be stupid not to do this, huh?" You say:

"I don't know if I would use the word stupid, but I do think you're smart to get this done. I'll go ahead and add it to the repair order."

If they don't stop you, they just bought! Sometimes it is just a matter of getting the customer to slow down and think about what they have said and what they are doing.

The "While That May Be True" Close

When your best customers, who in the past have bought nearly everything you have presented, say no to an obviously needed service or repair, they are telling you that they are confused. They are telling you that you have not presented a convincing argument. They may feel you are taking advantage of them given their past buying history. They need you to slow down and "court" them a bit. This is an easy situation to turn-around and if you use this *close,* you should expect a 98% *closing* ratio, or even higher.

After you have presented to the customer and they state something like: "I'm confused. I know this is a Chevrolet, but I have a Ford at home and it has about the same number of miles on it. When I took the Ford in for service last week at the Ford dealership, they didn't say anything about needing a service like this one. If I don't have to do this on my Ford, why would I have to do it on this vehicle?"

You answer with this:

"Mr./ Ms. Customer, I do not know why the Ford dealership down the road did not recommend this service. But what I can show you is why Chevrolet does."

You simply go over the benefits and features of the service and then follow with:

"Now that I have better explained this Mr./ Ms. Customer, I am sure you see the benefits and will want me to proceed, right?"

Remember, do not short-cut your best customers and take them for granted. You didn't win them over initially by giving incomplete explanations and rushing through presentations. Take your time, **Every Car, Every Time!**

The "Now vs. Later" Close

This *close* is essentially the very same as the *"The Long Run" close.* The only difference is that there are some slight word changes. It too will offer a 70% or higher effective *closing* ratio.

Why would I put two nearly identical *closes* in here? Because I want to show you that sometimes, just a slight word adjustment can finesse the presentation enough to make the sale. The *"Long Run" close* is used when someone says, "I think I will wait." The *"Now vs. Later"* close should be used when the customer says, "I will get it done later."

The difference? This customer is telling you that *they are going to do the service,* **later.** Once you begin to get into the psychology of selling, and you should, if you are serious about this profession, you will learn that the more you **mirror the customers' words and actions,** the more they will assume that you are just like them and you that you truly understand. The

"*Long-Run*" customer is telling you that they are going to **wait**. They are **not positive** if they are going to do it. The decision to buy has *not.*been made. However, the "*Now vs. Later*" customer is **going to buy**. The decision to buy has been made. **They are going to buy, later**. This slight and delicate difference requires that you make an adjustment that mirrors their intentions. By taking the same verbiage from the other *close* and changing it slightly, you will create a successful *close,* that otherwise might have failed. The focus is on the idea that the customer has told you **they are going to do it, just later.** Here, you lead them to the next step, presenting the case for why they need to do it **now**.

The *Close:*

"*Mr./Ms. Customer, is if you wish to do this service LATER you can, simply because it is your vehicle and your decision. But, let me point something out. Based on the number of miles you typically put on your vehicle in a month and your driving habits, by doing it later, or sometime in the next 90 days, you will continue to wear your tires until they completely wear- out. When that happens, you could be looking at a flat tire. Flat tires rarely happen in your driveway. New tires are about $____. A flat tire will not only mean new tires, but possible a tow bill, lost work, and compromised safety for you and your family. By getting tires today, in the long run, you will not only have peace-of mind-of knowing that your tires are fine, but also that you saved over*

$___ on a tow bill and possible lost work. That alone makes it worth reconsidering, wouldn't you agree?"

Same *close,* slightly different words for a slightly different customer. Same results. Many times, it's not what you say, but how you say it that counts.

NOTE: The *closes* presented here are not necessarily the best or the most important. They are simply the *closes* that I have seen work many times on many different service drives. With this selection, the intention was to provide you with a sample to define and create an understanding of **The Close.** The *closes* presented demonstrate the conditions, tone, and posture that can be assumed for customer presentations. I also wanted to show you the many factors that will dictate the type of *close* you select and what results you can expect.

The *closes* presented are enough to get any service advisor started on the path to becoming a *master closer.* Once you master these *closes,* I suggest you research more *closes* and add them to your portfolio. Whether you acquire these *closes* from my training or whether you discover them somewhere else, the goal remains the same, you must master as many as you can. You need to be prepared for any situation that arises on your service drive. Commit all *closes* to memory so that it becomes second nature to you. Ultimately, you don't want to hesitate and run through options in your head. You want your interactions to be seamless and flow naturally, without hesitation. When you have 100 *closes* committed to memory in your arsenal, you can begin to consider yourself one step closer becoming a master salesperson.

DELIVERING THE VEHICLE BACK TO YOUR CUSTOMER

The delivery of the vehicle back to the customer is a critical step in the sales process because it is typically the last thing the customer is likely to remember. Staying in control, taking your time, and being thorough are the key elements to a great delivery. It starts with the following word track:

"Mr./ Ms. Customer, this is _____ calling from _____. I am calling to let you know that your vehicle is ready when promised. Do you feel you could be here by 2:30 or would 2:40 be better for you.?" Keep giving additional choices until a time is agreed upon. *"Great! I will see you at 2:40 and I am positive that you will be pleased with the quality of service performed. Plan on it taking about ten minutes* (or however long it will take) *to get your vehicle, as I will want to spend a little time with you going over your repair order and fully explaining what services were performed on your vehicle today. Okay? Great, I will see you then."*

- The delivery when the guest is in the waiting room

- Paperwork is **completed and reviewed** for accuracy

- Advisor collects the guest from the waiting area and **escorts** them to the cashier

- Advisor **explains** all work completed and all charges if available **line- by-line**

- Advisor **reviews and advises** on the current vehicle's health report and advises what will be completed on the **next preventative maintenance service**

- Advisor asks the guest if they have any **questions** about their service visit

- Customer approves the paperwork and **remits payment** to the cashier if payment is due

- Advisor **reminds** their guest again about the **next visit check-in** that was scheduled during the check-in process to ensure customer retention

- Advisor **escorts the guest** to the vehicle, opens **the driver-side door and tells the guest that it was their utmost pleasure to have served them.** Advisor also asks if there was anything else that they could have done to exceed expectations.

Quite often, I am asked *not* to teach the advisors about **coaching for a survey** since most manufactures frown upon this. I am a firm believer that you **do not need to coach a customer into a survey** if you have completed a quality job and explained the benefits of services rendered to their vehicle.

The delivery of the vehicle when the guest is not a "waiter" and has dropped-off the vehicle

- Paperwork is **completed and reviewed** for accuracy

- Advisor **contacts guest and reviews work order** and all applicable charges

- Advisor **schedules** a pick-up time

- Guest arrives and the advisor **escorts** them to the cashiering station

- Advisor **explains** all work completed and all charges if available **line by line**

- Advisor **reviews and advises** on the current vehicle's health report and advises what will be completed on the **next preventative maintenance service**

- Advisor asks the guest if they have any **questions** about their service visit

- Customer approves the paperwork and **remits payment** to cashier if payment is due

- Advisor **reminds** their guest again about the **next visit check-in** that was scheduled during the write-up to ensure customer retention

- Advisor **escorts the guest** to the vehicle, **opens the driver-side door and tells the guest that it was their utmost pleasure to have served them.** The Advisor also asks if there was anything else they could have done to exceed expectations.

FOLLOW-UP AFTER A CUSTOMER VISIT

Why follow-up with your customers?

78% of customers who receive a handwritten thank you note and a follow-up telephone call will return for future service needs

20% will return and purchase the declined services within 48 hours of being ask to, if there is a followed-up and they are asked to do so

The "Three-Day Follow-Up Call" Word Track

"Mr./Ms. Customer, this is _____ from_____. Did I call at a good time? The reason I am calling is because you had your vehicle in here for service a few days ago and I wanted to make sure that you are happy and to see if the repair has completely solved your problems." Wait for response. If positive, proceed. If not, write down the complaint and take it to management. *"Great Mr./ Ms. Customer, I'm glad that your experience was good and I look*

*forward to seeing you during your **next visit**. Is there anything else that I can do for you right now? Thanks again!"*

The "Declined Services Call-Back" Word Track

"Hello, Mr./Ms. _____? I am calling this evening to follow-up on the work you had completed at our service department recently. Did I call at a good time? Great! When you were here, did you feel like everything went well? " If the customer responds, "no", tell them your manager will be contacting them. If "yes", go on. *"Great, I am glad that things went as you expected. That is always our goal. Also, while I was going through our paperwork, I noticed that there were a few things that we recommended for your vehicle that you declined to have done because you wanted to think about it. Have you had enough time to think it over and if so, would it be okay with you if I go ahead and get you on our schedule to get that work addressed?"* If yes, proceed with setting the check-in time and thank them for their business. If no, thank them for talking with you and tell them that you look forward to working with them when their next service is due.

The" Inviting Your Customer Back" Word Track

"Mr./Ms. Customer, this is ____ calling from_____. Did I call at a good time ?The reason I'm calling is because while going over my records, I discovered that it has been more than a year since you have had your vehicle in for service. Is everything

okay? Wait for response. *"Is there any reason you have not returned?"* Wait for response. If positive, proceed. If not, write down the complaint and take it to management.

"According to my records, you are behind on some of your required maintenance and I would like to set-up a check-in time for you to come in and get caught-up. What you need is _____. Explain what needs to be done. *"When would be a good time for you to come in? Would later this week or next week be better?"* Continue with alternate choices until you have a set a check-in time. Once you have a set check-in time, reconfirm and re-explain what you will be doing before hanging up. Also, give your name again.

NOTE: It is a great idea to send a handwritten note that thanks them for setting a check-in time and reminds them of the date and time, as well.

ANOTHER NOTE: Notice that I did not suggest texting or emailing your customers. Although I feel texting and emailing your customers is okay, it is *only* okay to use to provide updates and progress of the work being done. Texting and emailing should never be used to *close* a sale, ask for additional money, or to ask for additional time that may be needed. Again, texting and email your clients should only be used to update customers. When you text or email a customer, and ask for money or time, you surrender control because you cannot use your skill to judge things like body language, voice, and emotion.

Managing Your Daily Success

Managing your daily success can be very easily done by reviewing pre-written repair orders and/or by reviewing your scheduled check-in times the night before your customers arrive. The more you are prepared for your customers prior to their arrival, the more successful you will be.

Manager's perspective

Allows you to forecast - The goal is to identify the opportunity each advisor has with every customer *before* the customer arrives.

Allows for one-on-one time with your staff – One-on-one time will be the most valuable time you spend with your advisors each day.

Train your staff - If you foresee that an advisor has a tough situation scheduled for the next day, you can train and role-play with the advisor to prepare them for success.

Hold your staff accountable - Once you define expectations and both you and your staff understand what is possible with each customer, each day, holding them accountable to get what is possible becomes much easier.

Salesperson's perspective

Provides you with time to prepare for your customer – There are two types of customers:

A. Heat

B. Nice

Again, the more prepared you are the more successful you will be.

Keeps you on track to hit your goals - One of the secrets to meeting and exceeding your goals is knowing where you stand with them at all times.

Provides you with time to develop strategies - If you can recognize and identify potential difficult situations before they erupt, you can develop strategies in advance of coming face-to-face with the customer. This will allow you to be in control and steer the outcome in the desired direction.

Provides you with the ability to forecast results - This is the most valuable step in becoming a world-class salesperson. Knowing what is truly possible before you interact with your customers makes it much easier to be successful with each one.

The Daily Forecast Sheet

On I will deliver the following:

Number of Customers

Customer Paid Hours

Effective Labor Rate

Total Sales

Monthly Averages to Date:

Number of Customers % of Goal

Customer Paid Hours % of Goal

Effective Labor Rate % of Goal

Total Sales % of Goal

The End of Day Meeting

At the end of each day you should sit with your manager and or advisor and discuss the results of the day and compare that to the goals established the night before. Here is where a sharing of information will provide the truest picture of the progress of the day.

Manager's and Salesperson's Perspective

This collaboration is invaluable to the success of the entire organization.

1. Allows you to identify strengths and weakness

2. Gives you the opportunity to identify training needs

3. Gives you the opportunity to role-play

4. Reinforces strengths

5. Tells you where you are regarding your financial goals

6. Tells you how effective you/they are as a salesperson

SECURE THE OPPORTUNITY TO MAKE A PRESENTATION

Often, when you try to present extra products and services above and beyond what the customer is asking for, they instinctively **object before you even get the opportunity to make your presentation.** A basic fact in selling is that, if you cannot present your product, you cannot sell your product. That being the case, we must always set ourselves up to, at least, be able to make the presentation. The *closes* below are *closes*, but not in the normal sense. Where most *closes* end with you asking for the customer's money or business, **these *closes* are designed *only* to sell the customer on the idea of allowing you to make your presentation.** Again, if you cannot make the presentation, you cannot get the sale. Rest assured that these *closes* will not make you look pushy or like you are trying to sell something to a customer that they don't need. If delivered correctly and with the right tone, inflection in your voice, and body language, these *closes* will be seen as you trying to *help* the customer. So, the next time one of your customers' object before you get to make your presentation, use what follows:

The different closes and when to use them

"There is a Bad Economy" Close

"Mr./Ms. Customer, I know it's a tough economy. It has impacted me, my family, my neighbors, friends and just about everyone else. In times like these, everyone looks for ways to conserve, change spending habits, and save. While many things need to be put on hold, it is never wise to make your vehicle and it's maintenance one of those things. Your vehicle is an essential necessity. Having a vehicle that runs efficiently and without problems like unanticipated repairs is paramount in times like these. It is your vehicle that gets you to work and makes everything else possible."

NOTE: The customer will almost always respond with, "It sounds like you are talking about something really important. What is it?". When they ask that, they are now giving permission to make your presentation. Now you have a chance to *close* the deal.

"I Did Not Expect This" Close

"I know you did not expect news like this today, but it is imperative that, as we go over these items, you understand that it is not my job to upset you. It is my job to make sure that you fully understand your vehicle's needs and the importance of meeting those needs. Allow me to show you what I mean. If you agree with what I have to say and want us to get it done, that's great. If not,

at least you will know what your vehicle needs when you leave here today." Do not pause, but instead, make your presentation.

NOTE: Notice with this *close*, you are not waiting for the customer to "ask". This type of customer most likely will not ask, so you will need to be assertive, showing you are confident and in control. Your customers will love this.

"How to Save Money" Close

"The best way to save money in times like these is to ensure that you are always capable of getting to the place where your money is made. The only way to guarantee that this happens is to keep your vehicle properly and fully maintained, making any, and all needed repairs, no matter how large or small, as soon as possible."

NOTE: Again, the customer will almost always respond with, "It sounds like you are talking about something really important. What is it?" When they ask that, they are now giving you the go-ahead to make your presentation. Now you have a chance to *close* the deal.

"You Cannot Afford Not To" Close

*"Most of us can't afford to do many things that we took for granted in the past. However, I do know one thing that you cannot afford **not** to do and that is to not take care of your vehicle. Your vehicle is the backbone of your family and its security. So, as we review the needs of your vehicle today, let's not look at these items as simply spending money for the sake of spending money.*

Rather, you are investing in your vehicle, yourself, your family, and their security."

NOTE: With this *close,* since we brought the family into the equation, they will likely respond with, "I have to have a vehicle that is safe for me and my family. What is it that I need?" When they pose this question, they are now giving you the go-ahead to make your presentation. Now you have a chance to *close* the deal.

"It's Okay" Close

"Mr./Ms. Customer, it's okay. Most people walking in here today are in the same situation that you are in, including me. Things are tough, and who knows when all of this is going to end? But one thing I do know with certainty is that if you do not keep your vehicle and its needs at the top of the list, it will end up there anyway. The difference will be that when your vehicle's needs force their way to the top of the list, it will be because of expensive and untimely repairs that could have been easily prevented with considerably more affordable preventative maintenance. Let me show you what I mean."

NOTE: Just as before, with this *close* you will not wait for the customer to "ask". This type of customer most likely will not ask, so you will need to be assertive, showing that you are confident and in control. Your customer will love this.

ONE MORE THING...

Well there you have it. A guide to help you get started in one of the most exciting careers available today in North America. If you want a more comprehensive guide and course, please visit my website at thejeffcowan.com and sign up for my online courses. They cover everything included here plus much, much more and in greater detail. By investing in it, you will not only get substantially more information, but you will be tested as well. Once you pass the test, I will certify you and place your name on a list where we will be directing service mangers and shop owners to find you. On my site, you will also have the opportunity to enjoy and benefit from my other world class training courses as well.

For now, I thank you for the opportunity you have given me thus far to help you reach your career and financial goals. Please feel free to reach out to me anytime with any questions you may have. I am here to serve you and will serve you well.

Good Luck!

Jeff Cowan